A tropical rain forest is a very hot, wet place.

Rain forests are found all over the world, especially where the weather is warmest and rainiest.

A rain forest has three levels: the *canopy,* the *understory,* and the *ground layer.*

canopy

understory

ground layer

The top level, or canopy, is thick with leaves and branches. From above, it looks like a green blanket.

golden lion tamarin

Many animals find all they need to survive here without going down to the ground.

harpy eagle

passion-vine butterfly

The middle level, or understory, is home to a great variety of plants and animals.

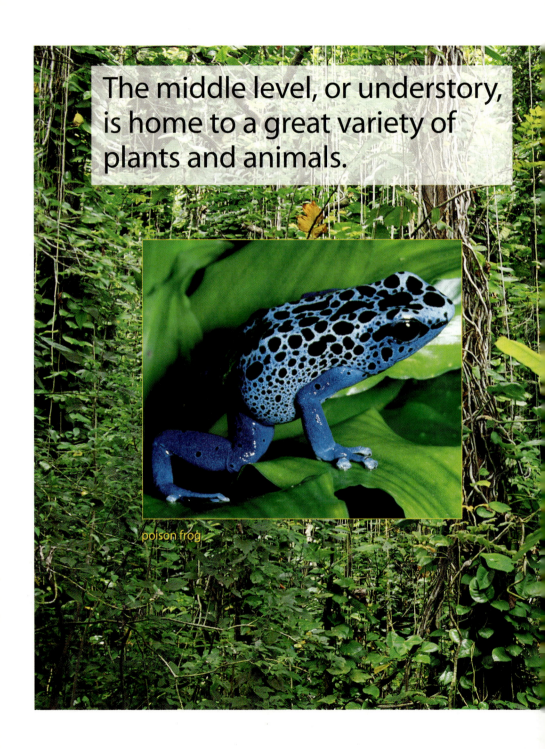

poison frog

They live among the lower, larger branches and tree trunks at this level.

slow loris

bromeliad

The ground layer includes the forest floor and its many rivers and streams.

jaguar

mushrooms

On this bottom level, the animals and plants live without much sunlight.

tamandua

leaf-cutter ants

Many people live and work in the world's rain forests.

Scientists study the many plants and animals. Plants from the rain forest are made into medicines.

Many foods come from the rain forest, such as bananas.

Scented oils from rain forest plants are used in important products, such as soap and candles.

Some things people do can harm the rain forest. Trees are cut down for wood.

The forest is burned for land to raise cattle and crops.

If we keep destroying the rain forest, it will no longer be there for anyone to live in or use.

Let's protect the rain forest for everyone.